50 Banana Recipes

By: Kelly Johnson

Table of Contents

- Banana Bread
- Banana Pancakes
- Banana Smoothie
- Banana Muffins
- Banana Pudding
- Banana Fritters
- Chocolate-Dipped Bananas
- Banana Nut Loaf
- Banana Ice Cream
- Banana Split
- Banana Oatmeal Cookies
- Banana Chocolate Chip Bread
- Banana Cream Pie
- Banana French Toast
- Banana Nutella Crepes
- Banana Chips
- Banana Coconut Energy Balls
- Banana Waffles
- Banana Brownies
- Banana Smoothie Bowl
- Peanut Butter Banana Sandwich
- Frozen Chocolate Bananas
- Banana Foster
- Banana Pudding Parfaits
- Banana Sorbet
- Banana Chia Pudding
- Baked Bananas with Cinnamon
- Banana and Peanut Butter Protein Bars
- Banana Nut Muffins
- Banana and Almond Butter Toast
- Banana Jam
- Banana Apple Crumble
- Banana and Walnut Cake
- Banana Avocado Smoothie
- Banana Flan

- Banana-Coconut Milk Popsicles
- Banana Mango Smoothie
- Banana Caramel Cake
- Banana and Chocolate Smoothie
- Banana Sorbet
- Grilled Banana Skewers
- Banana and Honey Yogurt Parfait
- Banana Cinnamon Rolls
- Vegan Banana Ice Cream
- Banana Coconut Milk Smoothie
- Banana and Strawberry Sorbet
- Banana Granola Bars
- Banana Rice Pudding
- Banana Chocolate Chip Muffins
- Banana Almond Smoothie

Banana Bread

Ingredients:

- 2-3 ripe bananas, mashed
- 1/3 cup melted butter
- 1 tsp baking soda
- Pinch of salt
- 3/4 cup sugar
- 1 beaten egg
- 1 tsp vanilla extract
- 1 1/2 cups all-purpose flour

Instructions:

1. Preheat the oven to 350°F (175°C) and grease a loaf pan.
2. In a mixing bowl, mash the bananas with a fork.
3. Stir the melted butter into the mashed bananas.
4. Mix in baking soda and salt.
5. Add sugar, beaten egg, and vanilla, and mix until well combined.
6. Stir in the flour until the mixture is smooth.
7. Pour the batter into the greased loaf pan and bake for 60-65 minutes, or until a toothpick comes out clean.
8. Let it cool before slicing and serving.

Banana Pancakes

Ingredients:

- 1 ripe banana, mashed
- 1 cup all-purpose flour
- 1 tbsp sugar
- 1 tsp baking powder
- 1/2 tsp baking soda
- Pinch of salt
- 3/4 cup milk
- 1 egg
- 2 tbsp melted butter
- 1 tsp vanilla extract

Instructions:

1. In a large bowl, combine flour, sugar, baking powder, baking soda, and salt.
2. In a separate bowl, whisk together the mashed banana, milk, egg, melted butter, and vanilla extract.
3. Pour the wet ingredients into the dry ingredients and stir until combined.
4. Heat a non-stick skillet over medium heat and lightly grease it with butter or oil.
5. Pour 1/4 cup of batter onto the skillet for each pancake and cook until bubbles form on the surface. Flip and cook for another 1-2 minutes.
6. Serve with maple syrup or your favorite toppings.

Banana Smoothie

Ingredients:

- 1 ripe banana
- 1 cup milk (or non-dairy milk)
- 1/2 cup Greek yogurt
- 1 tbsp honey (optional)
- Ice cubes (optional)

Instructions:

1. Combine all ingredients in a blender.
2. Blend until smooth and creamy.
3. Pour into a glass and serve immediately.

Banana Muffins

Ingredients:

- 2 ripe bananas, mashed
- 1 1/2 cups all-purpose flour
- 1/2 cup sugar
- 1/2 tsp baking soda
- 1/2 tsp baking powder
- 1/4 tsp salt
- 1/3 cup melted butter
- 1 egg
- 1 tsp vanilla extract

Instructions:

1. Preheat the oven to 350°F (175°C) and line a muffin tin with paper liners.
2. In a bowl, mix the mashed bananas with melted butter.
3. Stir in the egg and vanilla extract.
4. In another bowl, combine flour, sugar, baking soda, baking powder, and salt.
5. Fold the dry ingredients into the wet ingredients until just combined.
6. Spoon the batter into the muffin tin and bake for 18-20 minutes or until a toothpick comes out clean.
7. Let the muffins cool before serving.

Banana Pudding

Ingredients:

- 3 ripe bananas, sliced
- 1 box vanilla pudding mix
- 2 cups milk
- 1 cup whipped cream
- 1/2 cup vanilla wafer cookies, crushed

Instructions:

1. Prepare the vanilla pudding mix according to the package instructions using the milk.
2. In a trifle dish or serving bowl, layer the sliced bananas, pudding, whipped cream, and crushed vanilla wafer cookies.
3. Repeat the layers until all ingredients are used.
4. Chill in the refrigerator for at least 2 hours before serving.

Banana Fritters

Ingredients:

- 2 ripe bananas, mashed
- 1 cup all-purpose flour
- 1/4 cup sugar
- 1 tsp baking powder
- Pinch of salt
- 1/2 tsp vanilla extract
- 1/4 cup milk
- Oil for frying

Instructions:

1. In a bowl, combine the mashed bananas, flour, sugar, baking powder, salt, vanilla extract, and milk to form a batter.
2. Heat oil in a frying pan over medium heat.
3. Drop spoonfuls of the batter into the hot oil and fry until golden brown on both sides.
4. Drain the fritters on paper towels and serve warm with powdered sugar or honey.

Chocolate-Dipped Bananas

Ingredients:

- 2 ripe bananas, sliced into 1-inch pieces
- 1 cup dark chocolate chips
- 1 tsp coconut oil (optional)

Instructions:

1. Melt the chocolate chips in a heatproof bowl over a pot of simmering water or in the microwave, stirring every 30 seconds.
2. Dip each banana slice into the melted chocolate and place it on a parchment-lined baking sheet.
3. Refrigerate for 30 minutes or until the chocolate hardens.
4. Serve immediately or store in the fridge for later.

Banana Nut Loaf

Ingredients:

- 3 ripe bananas, mashed
- 1/3 cup melted butter
- 1/2 cup sugar
- 1 egg, beaten
- 1 tsp vanilla extract
- 1 tsp baking soda
- Pinch of salt
- 1 1/2 cups all-purpose flour
- 1/2 cup chopped walnuts (optional)

Instructions:

1. Preheat the oven to 350°F (175°C) and grease a loaf pan.
2. In a bowl, mix the mashed bananas with melted butter.
3. Stir in the sugar, beaten egg, and vanilla extract.
4. Add baking soda, salt, and flour, and mix until smooth.
5. Fold in chopped walnuts (if using).
6. Pour the batter into the loaf pan and bake for 60-65 minutes, or until a toothpick comes out clean.

Banana Ice Cream

Ingredients:

- 2 ripe bananas, sliced and frozen
- 1/2 tsp vanilla extract (optional)

Instructions:

1. Freeze the banana slices for at least 2 hours or overnight.
2. Blend the frozen banana slices in a food processor until smooth and creamy.
3. Optionally, add vanilla extract for flavor.
4. Serve immediately for soft-serve texture or freeze for a firmer consistency.

Banana Split

Ingredients:

- 2 ripe bananas, sliced lengthwise
- 3 scoops vanilla ice cream
- 3 scoops chocolate ice cream
- Chocolate syrup
- Caramel syrup
- Whipped cream
- Maraschino cherries
- Chopped nuts (optional)

Instructions:

1. Place the sliced bananas in a long dish.
2. Arrange one scoop each of vanilla and chocolate ice cream on top of the bananas.
3. Drizzle with chocolate and caramel syrup.
4. Top with whipped cream and maraschino cherries.
5. Sprinkle chopped nuts over the top if desired.
6. Serve immediately and enjoy!

Banana Oatmeal Cookies

Ingredients:

- 1 ripe banana, mashed
- 1 cup old-fashioned rolled oats
- 1/4 cup flour
- 1/4 cup brown sugar
- 1/4 cup raisins or chocolate chips (optional)
- 1/2 tsp cinnamon
- 1/4 tsp baking soda
- 1/4 tsp salt
- 1/4 cup melted butter or coconut oil
- 1/2 tsp vanilla extract

Instructions:

1. Preheat the oven to 350°F (175°C) and line a baking sheet with parchment paper.
2. In a bowl, mix the mashed banana, oats, flour, brown sugar, cinnamon, baking soda, salt, melted butter, and vanilla extract.
3. Stir in raisins or chocolate chips if desired.
4. Drop spoonfuls of the dough onto the baking sheet.
5. Bake for 8-10 minutes, or until golden brown.
6. Let the cookies cool on a wire rack.

Banana Chocolate Chip Bread

Ingredients:

- 3 ripe bananas, mashed
- 2 cups all-purpose flour
- 1 tsp baking soda
- 1/4 tsp salt
- 1/2 cup sugar
- 1/2 cup brown sugar
- 1/2 cup butter, melted
- 2 eggs, beaten
- 1 tsp vanilla extract
- 1 cup mini chocolate chips

Instructions:

1. Preheat the oven to 350°F (175°C) and grease a loaf pan.
2. In a bowl, combine the mashed bananas, melted butter, sugar, brown sugar, eggs, and vanilla extract.
3. In another bowl, mix the flour, baking soda, and salt.
4. Add the dry ingredients to the wet ingredients and stir until combined.
5. Gently fold in the chocolate chips.
6. Pour the batter into the loaf pan and bake for 60-65 minutes, or until a toothpick comes out clean.
7. Let the bread cool before slicing.

Banana Cream Pie

Ingredients:

- 1 pre-made pie crust (or homemade)
- 3 ripe bananas, sliced
- 1 box vanilla pudding mix
- 2 cups milk
- 1 cup heavy cream
- 1/4 cup powdered sugar
- 1 tsp vanilla extract

Instructions:

1. Prepare the vanilla pudding according to package instructions with 2 cups of milk.
2. Once the pudding has set, layer the sliced bananas into the pie crust.
3. Pour the pudding over the bananas and smooth the top.
4. Whip the heavy cream with powdered sugar and vanilla extract until stiff peaks form.
5. Spread the whipped cream on top of the pudding layer.
6. Chill the pie in the refrigerator for at least 2 hours before serving.

Banana French Toast

Ingredients:

- 2 ripe bananas, mashed
- 2 eggs
- 1/2 cup milk
- 1 tsp vanilla extract
- 4 slices of bread
- Butter for cooking
- Maple syrup
- Powdered sugar (optional)

Instructions:

1. In a bowl, whisk together the mashed bananas, eggs, milk, and vanilla extract.
2. Heat a pan or griddle over medium heat and add a little butter.
3. Dip each slice of bread into the banana mixture, making sure both sides are coated.
4. Cook the bread on the pan until golden brown on both sides, about 2-3 minutes per side.
5. Serve with maple syrup and powdered sugar if desired.

Banana Nutella Crepes

Ingredients:

- 1/2 cup Nutella
- 2 ripe bananas, sliced
- 8-10 crepes (store-bought or homemade)
- Powdered sugar for dusting

Instructions:

1. Warm the crepes in a skillet over medium heat for 30 seconds on each side.
2. Spread a thin layer of Nutella on one half of each crepe.
3. Add the sliced bananas on top of the Nutella.
4. Fold the crepes in half and serve with a dusting of powdered sugar.

Banana Chips

Ingredients:

- 2 ripe bananas, sliced thinly
- 1 tbsp lemon juice
- 1 tbsp coconut oil, melted (optional)
- Salt (optional)

Instructions:

1. Preheat the oven to 200°F (93°C) and line a baking sheet with parchment paper.
2. In a bowl, toss the banana slices with lemon juice and melted coconut oil.
3. Arrange the banana slices in a single layer on the baking sheet.
4. Bake for 1-2 hours, flipping the banana slices halfway through.
5. Once crispy, remove from the oven and sprinkle with salt if desired.

Banana Coconut Energy Balls

Ingredients:

- 1 ripe banana, mashed
- 1 cup rolled oats
- 1/4 cup shredded coconut
- 1/4 cup almond butter or peanut butter
- 1 tbsp honey
- 1/4 tsp cinnamon
- 1/4 tsp vanilla extract

Instructions:

1. In a bowl, mix the mashed banana, oats, shredded coconut, almond butter, honey, cinnamon, and vanilla extract.
2. Roll the mixture into small balls (about 1 inch in diameter).
3. Refrigerate for at least 30 minutes to firm up.
4. Store in an airtight container and enjoy as a snack.

Banana Waffles

Ingredients:

- 2 ripe bananas, mashed
- 2 cups all-purpose flour
- 2 tbsp sugar
- 2 tsp baking powder
- 1/2 tsp salt
- 2 large eggs
- 1 cup milk
- 1/4 cup melted butter
- 1 tsp vanilla extract

Instructions:

1. Preheat your waffle iron.
2. In a bowl, whisk together the flour, sugar, baking powder, and salt.
3. In another bowl, mix the mashed bananas, eggs, milk, melted butter, and vanilla extract.
4. Combine the wet and dry ingredients until smooth.
5. Pour the batter into the preheated waffle iron and cook according to the manufacturer's instructions.
6. Serve warm with your favorite toppings like syrup, fruit, or whipped cream.

Banana Brownies

Ingredients:

- 2 ripe bananas, mashed
- 1/2 cup butter, melted
- 1 cup sugar
- 1 tsp vanilla extract
- 2 large eggs
- 1 1/2 cups all-purpose flour
- 1/2 cup cocoa powder
- 1/2 tsp baking powder
- 1/4 tsp salt
- 1/2 cup chocolate chips (optional)

Instructions:

1. Preheat the oven to 350°F (175°C) and grease a baking dish.
2. In a large bowl, mix the mashed bananas, melted butter, sugar, and vanilla extract.
3. Add the eggs one at a time, mixing well after each addition.
4. In another bowl, combine the flour, cocoa powder, baking powder, and salt.
5. Gradually add the dry ingredients to the wet ingredients, stirring until just combined.
6. Stir in the chocolate chips if desired.
7. Pour the batter into the prepared dish and bake for 25-30 minutes, or until a toothpick comes out clean.
8. Let cool before slicing.

Banana Smoothie Bowl

Ingredients:

- 2 ripe bananas, frozen
- 1/2 cup Greek yogurt
- 1/2 cup almond milk or regular milk
- 1 tbsp honey or maple syrup
- Toppings: granola, sliced banana, chia seeds, coconut flakes, or nuts

Instructions:

1. In a blender, combine the frozen bananas, Greek yogurt, almond milk, and honey. Blend until smooth.
2. Pour the smoothie into a bowl.
3. Top with your favorite toppings, such as granola, extra banana slices, chia seeds, or coconut flakes.
4. Serve immediately and enjoy!

Peanut Butter Banana Sandwich

Ingredients:

- 2 slices whole grain bread
- 2 tbsp peanut butter
- 1 ripe banana, sliced

Instructions:

1. Spread the peanut butter evenly on one side of each slice of bread.
2. Layer the banana slices on top of one slice of bread.
3. Top with the second slice of bread to form a sandwich.
4. Serve immediately or cut into halves for easier eating.

Frozen Chocolate Bananas

Ingredients:

- 2 ripe bananas, sliced into rounds
- 1 cup dark chocolate chips
- 1 tbsp coconut oil
- 1/4 cup chopped nuts or sprinkles (optional)

Instructions:

1. Line a baking sheet with parchment paper and arrange the banana slices in a single layer.
2. In a microwave-safe bowl, melt the chocolate chips and coconut oil together, stirring every 30 seconds until smooth.
3. Dip each banana slice into the melted chocolate and return it to the baking sheet.
4. Sprinkle with chopped nuts or sprinkles if desired.
5. Freeze for at least 2 hours or until the chocolate is hardened.
6. Enjoy as a frozen treat!

Banana Foster

Ingredients:

- 2 ripe bananas, sliced
- 1/4 cup butter
- 1/2 cup brown sugar
- 1/4 cup dark rum
- 1/2 tsp cinnamon
- 1/4 tsp nutmeg
- Vanilla ice cream (for serving)

Instructions:

1. In a skillet over medium heat, melt the butter.
2. Add the brown sugar, cinnamon, and nutmeg, stirring until the sugar dissolves and the sauce thickens.
3. Add the banana slices and cook for 2-3 minutes until they soften.
4. Carefully add the rum and ignite with a long lighter (optional for flambe).
5. Let the flames subside, then serve the banana mixture over vanilla ice cream.
6. Enjoy this decadent dessert!

Banana Pudding Parfaits

Ingredients:

- 2 ripe bananas, sliced
- 1 box vanilla pudding mix
- 2 cups milk
- 1 1/2 cups whipped cream
- 1/2 box vanilla wafers

Instructions:

1. Prepare the vanilla pudding according to the package instructions using milk.
2. In a glass or dessert dish, layer the pudding, banana slices, and vanilla wafers.
3. Top with whipped cream and repeat the layers.
4. Finish with a layer of whipped cream and a few banana slices on top.
5. Chill for at least an hour before serving.

Banana Sorbet

Ingredients:

- 4 ripe bananas, sliced and frozen
- 1/4 cup honey or agave syrup (optional)
- 1 tsp lemon juice

Instructions:

1. Place the frozen banana slices in a food processor.
2. Blend until smooth, scraping down the sides as necessary.
3. Add honey or agave syrup and lemon juice and blend again.
4. Serve immediately for a soft-serve consistency or freeze for a firmer sorbet.

Banana Chia Pudding

Ingredients:

- 2 ripe bananas, mashed
- 1/2 cup chia seeds
- 1 1/2 cups almond milk or regular milk
- 1 tbsp maple syrup (optional)
- 1/2 tsp vanilla extract

Instructions:

1. In a bowl, combine the mashed bananas, chia seeds, almond milk, maple syrup, and vanilla extract.
2. Stir well to combine and let sit in the refrigerator for at least 4 hours or overnight.
3. Serve chilled, topped with sliced bananas or your favorite fruit.

Baked Bananas with Cinnamon

Ingredients:

- 2 ripe bananas, halved lengthwise
- 1 tbsp butter, melted
- 1 tbsp honey
- 1/2 tsp ground cinnamon

Instructions:

1. Preheat the oven to 350°F (175°C).
2. Place the banana halves in a baking dish, cut side up.
3. Drizzle the melted butter and honey over the bananas, then sprinkle with cinnamon.
4. Bake for 10-12 minutes, or until the bananas are soft and caramelized.
5. Serve warm as a delicious dessert or snack.

Banana and Peanut Butter Protein Bars

Ingredients:

- 2 ripe bananas, mashed
- 1/2 cup peanut butter
- 1 cup rolled oats
- 1/4 cup protein powder (vanilla or chocolate)
- 1/4 cup honey or maple syrup
- 1/2 tsp vanilla extract
- A pinch of salt

Instructions:

1. Preheat the oven to 350°F (175°C) and line a baking dish with parchment paper.
2. In a bowl, mix together the mashed bananas, peanut butter, honey, and vanilla extract until smooth.
3. Add the oats, protein powder, and salt. Stir until combined.
4. Pour the mixture into the prepared baking dish and press it into an even layer.
5. Bake for 15-18 minutes or until golden and firm to the touch.
6. Let cool before cutting into bars.

Banana Nut Muffins

Ingredients:

- 2 ripe bananas, mashed
- 1/2 cup sugar (or honey)
- 1/4 cup vegetable oil
- 2 eggs
- 1 1/2 cups all-purpose flour
- 1/2 tsp baking soda
- 1/4 tsp salt
- 1/2 cup chopped walnuts (or your favorite nuts)
- 1 tsp vanilla extract

Instructions:

1. Preheat the oven to 350°F (175°C) and grease or line a muffin tin.
2. In a bowl, mix the mashed bananas, sugar, oil, eggs, and vanilla extract.
3. In another bowl, combine the flour, baking soda, and salt.
4. Gradually add the dry ingredients to the wet mixture, stirring until just combined.
5. Fold in the chopped walnuts.
6. Divide the batter evenly among the muffin cups.
7. Bake for 18-22 minutes, or until a toothpick comes out clean.
8. Cool in the tin for a few minutes before transferring to a wire rack.

Banana and Almond Butter Toast

Ingredients:

- 2 slices whole-grain bread
- 2 tbsp almond butter
- 1 ripe banana, sliced
- A sprinkle of cinnamon

Instructions:

1. Toast the slices of bread to your liking.
2. Spread the almond butter evenly on each slice of toast.
3. Arrange the banana slices on top of the almond butter.
4. Sprinkle with cinnamon and serve immediately.

Banana Jam

Ingredients:

- 4 ripe bananas, mashed
- 1/4 cup lemon juice
- 1/4 cup sugar (or sweetener of choice)
- 1 tbsp pectin (optional, for thicker consistency)

Instructions:

1. In a saucepan, combine the mashed bananas, lemon juice, and sugar.
2. Heat over medium heat, stirring occasionally, until the mixture begins to simmer.
3. If desired, add pectin to thicken and continue to cook for 5-10 minutes.
4. Let cool and transfer to jars for storage. Refrigerate and use within a week.

Banana Apple Crumble

Ingredients:

- 2 ripe bananas, sliced
- 2 apples, peeled and sliced
- 1/4 cup brown sugar
- 1 tsp cinnamon
- 1 cup oats
- 1/2 cup flour
- 1/4 cup melted butter
- 1/4 cup chopped walnuts (optional)

Instructions:

1. Preheat the oven to 350°F (175°C).
2. In a bowl, combine the bananas and apples with brown sugar and cinnamon.
3. In another bowl, mix the oats, flour, melted butter, and chopped walnuts.
4. Spread the fruit mixture in a greased baking dish.
5. Top with the oat crumble mixture and bake for 25-30 minutes, or until golden and bubbly.
6. Serve warm with a scoop of vanilla ice cream or whipped cream.

Banana and Walnut Cake

Ingredients:

- 2 ripe bananas, mashed
- 1/2 cup butter, softened
- 1 cup sugar
- 2 eggs
- 1 1/2 cups all-purpose flour
- 1/2 tsp baking soda
- 1/4 tsp salt
- 1/2 cup chopped walnuts
- 1 tsp vanilla extract

Instructions:

1. Preheat the oven to 350°F (175°C) and grease a cake pan.
2. In a bowl, cream together the butter and sugar.
3. Add the eggs and mashed bananas, and mix until smooth.
4. In a separate bowl, whisk together the flour, baking soda, and salt.
5. Gradually add the dry ingredients to the wet mixture and mix until combined.
6. Fold in the chopped walnuts.
7. Pour the batter into the prepared pan and bake for 30-35 minutes or until a toothpick comes out clean.
8. Let cool before slicing.

Banana Avocado Smoothie

Ingredients:

- 1 ripe banana
- 1/2 avocado
- 1 cup almond milk (or regular milk)
- 1 tbsp honey or sweetener of choice
- A pinch of cinnamon (optional)

Instructions:

1. Combine the banana, avocado, almond milk, and honey in a blender.
2. Blend until smooth and creamy.
3. Pour into a glass, sprinkle with cinnamon, and serve immediately.

Banana Flan

Ingredients:

- 3 ripe bananas, mashed
- 1 can sweetened condensed milk
- 1 cup whole milk
- 4 large eggs
- 1 tsp vanilla extract
- 1/2 cup sugar (for caramelizing)

Instructions:

1. Preheat the oven to 350°F (175°C).
2. In a saucepan, melt the sugar over medium heat to create caramel, swirling it in the pan to ensure even coloring. Pour the caramel into the bottom of a baking dish and set aside to cool.
3. In a blender, combine the mashed bananas, sweetened condensed milk, whole milk, eggs, and vanilla extract. Blend until smooth.
4. Pour the banana mixture over the caramelized sugar in the baking dish.
5. Bake for 50-60 minutes, or until the flan is set and a toothpick comes out clean.
6. Let cool before inverting onto a plate and serving.

Banana-Coconut Milk Popsicles

Ingredients:

- 2 ripe bananas, mashed
- 1 cup coconut milk
- 1/4 cup honey or maple syrup
- 1/2 tsp vanilla extract

Instructions:

1. In a bowl, mix the mashed bananas, coconut milk, honey, and vanilla extract.
2. Pour the mixture into popsicle molds.
3. Freeze for at least 4 hours or until solid.
4. Unmold and serve.

Banana Mango Smoothie

Ingredients:

- 1 ripe banana
- 1/2 cup mango chunks (fresh or frozen)
- 1/2 cup almond milk (or regular milk)
- 1 tbsp honey (optional)

Instructions:

1. Combine the banana, mango, almond milk, and honey in a blender.
2. Blend until smooth and creamy.
3. Pour into a glass and serve immediately.

Banana Caramel Cake

Ingredients:

- 2 ripe bananas, mashed
- 1/2 cup butter, softened
- 1 cup brown sugar
- 2 eggs
- 1 1/2 cups all-purpose flour
- 1 tsp baking powder
- 1/2 tsp baking soda
- 1/4 tsp salt
- 1 tsp vanilla extract
- 1/2 cup caramel sauce

Instructions:

1. Preheat the oven to 350°F (175°C) and grease a cake pan.
2. In a bowl, cream together the butter and brown sugar.
3. Add the eggs and mashed bananas, mixing until smooth.
4. In a separate bowl, whisk together the flour, baking powder, baking soda, and salt.
5. Gradually add the dry ingredients to the wet mixture, stirring until combined.
6. Add vanilla extract and mix well.
7. Pour the batter into the prepared pan and bake for 30-35 minutes or until a toothpick comes out clean.
8. Let the cake cool, then drizzle with caramel sauce before serving.

Banana and Chocolate Smoothie

Ingredients:

- 1 ripe banana
- 1/2 cup milk (or dairy-free milk)
- 2 tbsp cocoa powder
- 1 tbsp honey or sweetener of choice
- 1/4 cup Greek yogurt (optional for creaminess)
- A handful of ice cubes

Instructions:

1. Place the banana, milk, cocoa powder, honey, and ice cubes into a blender.
2. Blend until smooth.
3. If you want a creamier texture, add Greek yogurt and blend again.
4. Pour into a glass and serve immediately.

Banana Sorbet

Ingredients:

- 4 ripe bananas, sliced
- 1 tbsp lemon juice
- 2 tbsp honey or maple syrup
- A pinch of salt

Instructions:

1. Freeze the banana slices for at least 4 hours or overnight.
2. Once frozen, place the banana slices in a food processor along with lemon juice, honey, and a pinch of salt.
3. Blend until smooth and creamy.
4. Serve immediately as soft serve or freeze for an additional hour to firm it up.

Grilled Banana Skewers

Ingredients:

- 4 ripe bananas, cut into chunks
- 2 tbsp honey
- 1 tsp cinnamon
- Skewers (wooden or metal)

Instructions:

1. Preheat the grill to medium heat.
2. Thread the banana chunks onto the skewers.
3. In a small bowl, mix the honey and cinnamon together.
4. Brush the banana skewers with the honey-cinnamon mixture.
5. Grill the skewers for about 2-3 minutes on each side, until golden and caramelized.
6. Serve immediately as a sweet dessert or snack.

Banana and Honey Yogurt Parfait

Ingredients:

- 2 ripe bananas, sliced
- 1 cup Greek yogurt
- 2 tbsp honey
- 1/4 cup granola
- A few mint leaves for garnish (optional)

Instructions:

1. Layer the Greek yogurt, honey, and banana slices in a glass or bowl.
2. Top with granola and garnish with mint leaves.
3. Serve as a healthy breakfast or snack.

Banana Cinnamon Rolls

Ingredients:

- 1 package (2 1/4 tsp) active dry yeast
- 1/4 cup warm water
- 1/2 cup milk
- 1/2 cup sugar
- 1/2 cup butter, melted
- 1 ripe banana, mashed
- 3 cups all-purpose flour
- 1/2 tsp salt
- 1 tsp cinnamon
- 1/2 cup brown sugar
- 1/4 cup butter, softened

Instructions:

1. In a bowl, combine the warm water, yeast, and a pinch of sugar. Let sit for 5 minutes to activate.
2. In a large mixing bowl, combine the milk, sugar, melted butter, and mashed banana.
3. Add the yeast mixture, flour, and salt. Mix until a dough forms.
4. Knead the dough on a floured surface for about 5 minutes.
5. Place the dough in a greased bowl, cover with a towel, and let rise for about 1 hour.
6. Preheat the oven to 350°F (175°C). Punch down the dough and roll it out into a rectangle.
7. Mix cinnamon and brown sugar, then spread the softened butter on the dough. Sprinkle the cinnamon-sugar mixture on top.
8. Roll the dough into a log and slice into 12 rolls.
9. Place the rolls in a greased pan and bake for 20-25 minutes or until golden.
10. Serve warm, optionally drizzled with icing.

Vegan Banana Ice Cream

Ingredients:

- 4 ripe bananas, sliced
- 1/2 tsp vanilla extract
- 1/4 cup coconut milk or almond milk

Instructions:

1. Freeze the banana slices for at least 4 hours or overnight.
2. Once frozen, place the banana slices in a food processor with vanilla extract and milk.
3. Blend until smooth and creamy.
4. Serve immediately as soft-serve or freeze for an additional hour to firm up.

Banana Coconut Milk Smoothie

Ingredients:

- 1 ripe banana
- 1/2 cup coconut milk
- 1/2 cup almond milk (or any other milk of choice)
- 1 tbsp honey or sweetener of choice
- A handful of ice cubes

Instructions:

1. Place the banana, coconut milk, almond milk, honey, and ice cubes into a blender.
2. Blend until smooth.
3. Pour into a glass and serve immediately.

Banana and Strawberry Sorbet

Ingredients:

- 3 ripe bananas, sliced
- 1 cup strawberries, hulled and sliced
- 2 tbsp honey or maple syrup
- 1 tbsp lemon juice

Instructions:

1. Freeze the banana slices and strawberries for at least 4 hours or overnight.
2. Place the frozen fruit, honey, and lemon juice in a food processor or blender.
3. Blend until smooth and creamy.
4. Serve immediately as a soft-serve or freeze for an hour to firm up for a scoopable texture.

Banana Granola Bars

Ingredients:

- 2 ripe bananas, mashed
- 2 cups rolled oats
- 1/2 cup nut butter (peanut, almond, etc.)
- 1/4 cup honey or maple syrup
- 1/4 cup raisins or dried fruit (optional)
- 1/4 cup nuts or seeds (optional)
- 1 tsp vanilla extract
- 1/2 tsp cinnamon

Instructions:

1. Preheat the oven to 350°F (175°C) and line a baking dish with parchment paper.
2. In a large bowl, mix the mashed bananas, nut butter, honey, vanilla, and cinnamon.
3. Stir in the oats, raisins, and nuts or seeds if using.
4. Pour the mixture into the prepared baking dish and press it down evenly.
5. Bake for 20-25 minutes, or until golden brown.
6. Let cool before cutting into bars. Store in an airtight container.

Banana Rice Pudding

Ingredients:

- 1 ripe banana, mashed
- 1 cup cooked rice
- 1 1/2 cups milk (or dairy-free milk)
- 1/4 cup sugar or sweetener of choice
- 1 tsp vanilla extract
- 1/2 tsp ground cinnamon
- A pinch of salt

Instructions:

1. In a medium saucepan, combine the cooked rice, milk, sugar, vanilla, cinnamon, and salt.
2. Bring to a simmer over medium heat and cook, stirring frequently, until the mixture thickens (about 10-15 minutes).
3. Stir in the mashed banana and cook for another 2-3 minutes, until well combined.
4. Serve warm or chilled, topped with extra cinnamon or fruit if desired.

Banana Chocolate Chip Muffins

Ingredients:

- 2 ripe bananas, mashed
- 1 1/2 cups all-purpose flour
- 1/2 cup sugar or sweetener of choice
- 1 tsp baking soda
- 1/2 tsp baking powder
- 1/4 tsp salt
- 1/2 cup chocolate chips
- 1/4 cup vegetable oil or melted butter
- 2 large eggs
- 1 tsp vanilla extract

Instructions:

1. Preheat the oven to 350°F (175°C) and line a muffin tin with paper liners.
2. In a large bowl, mix the mashed bananas, eggs, oil, and vanilla extract.
3. In a separate bowl, combine the flour, sugar, baking soda, baking powder, and salt.
4. Add the dry ingredients to the wet ingredients and stir until just combined.
5. Fold in the chocolate chips.
6. Spoon the batter into the muffin tin, filling each cup about 3/4 full.
7. Bake for 18-20 minutes, or until a toothpick inserted into the center comes out clean.
8. Let cool before serving.

Banana Almond Smoothie

Ingredients:

- 1 ripe banana
- 1/4 cup almond butter
- 1/2 cup almond milk (or any milk of choice)
- 1 tbsp honey or maple syrup
- A pinch of cinnamon
- A handful of ice cubes

Instructions:

1. Place the banana, almond butter, almond milk, honey, cinnamon, and ice cubes into a blender.
2. Blend until smooth and creamy.
3. Pour into a glass and serve immediately.

www.ingramcontent.com/pod-product-compliance
Lightning Source LLC
LaVergne TN
LVHW081331060526
838201LV00055B/2573